LOST BALLS

LOST BALL IN THE ROUGH, 18TH HOLE, BANDON DUNES GOLF RESORT, BANDON, OREGON

LOST BALLS

Great Holes, Tough Shots, and Bad Lies

CHARLES LINDSAY

FOREWORD BY **JOHN UPDIKE**

"BETWEEN NINES" BY **GREG NORMAN**

BULFINCH PRESS

NEW YORK | BOSTON | LONDON

BULFINCH PRESS

HACHETTE BOOK GROUP USA
237 PART AVENUE, NEW YORK, NY 10017
VISIT OUR WEB SITE AT WWW.BULFINCHPRESS.COM

FIRST EDITION
THIRD PRINTING, 2008

ISBN 978-0-8212-6185-9
LIBRARY OF CONGRESS CONTROL NUMBER 2004114548

DESIGNED BY MIKO McGINTY

PRINTED IN SINGAPORE

Lost Balls is dedicated to the greens keepers, pros, historians, collectors, and golfing friends who were so helpful in the making of this book.

John Updike

And the wind shall say: "Here were decent
  godless people:
Their only monument the asphalt road
And a thousand lost golf balls."

            —T. S. Eliot, chorus to *The Rock*

I have seen news videos of outfielders rummaging for a baseball lost in the ivy on the quaintly leafy wall at Wrigley Field, and I have experienced mis-hit tennis balls flying over the court fence deep into an impenetrable grove beyond; but no sport offers the sensation of lostness as often and enragingly as does golf. The damn thing *has* to be here, we think as we thrash at a clump of blueberry bushes or buffalo grass with the 7-iron we hopefully brought with us into the wilderness. Our obliging partners tramp in circles with us for a few minutes, peeking into drainage ditches and under fallen palm fronds, but their hearts aren't in it the way

ours are; this lost ball represents two strokes, and two extra strokes could mean the hole and even, it could be, the match, the entire outing, the day itself. *Why me?* one wonders. It was just a little slice, a tiny tail probably induced by the wind. It carried only a tad, a mere yard or two, into the woods, or the marsh, or the tall grass. Why couldn't it have been the other fellow, the loudmouth buddy smugly announcing, "O.K., we've given it five minutes, let's get a move on. It's getting dark, guys"? Not as dark, actually, as the inner weather as one trudges along, dragging like the foursome's crippled foot, "out of the hole" as they say, headed for an ignominious triple bogey, a condescending, token "paper seven."

The whereabouts of the ball are in a sense the key to every ball game, but the whereabouts are most picturesque in golf. Tangles of running raspberry, shadowy depths of a deep sand bunker,

JOHN UPDIKE TAKING A PENALTY DROP FROM AN UNPLAYABLE LIE, SALEM COUNTRY CLUB, PEABODY, MASSACHUSETTS

CIRCA 1900 *BRAMBLE* BALL WITH LADYBUGS, FOUND IN AN UNDISCLOSED GOLF-BALL HUNTING GROUND

sandy beds of shallow little watercress-choked creeks, weedy lees of lichen-laden stone walls, snake-infested moonscapes of pre-Cambrian basalt just off the plush watered fairways of a desert course, the pulpy flesh of a venerable saguaro cactus, the leaf-mulched floor of a hushed beech forest, the squishy tummocks of a reedy marsh, the hot and sere macadam of the club parking lot, the concrete curb next to the snack shop, the bed of petunias and pansies lifted up on creosoted railroad ties beside the eleventh tee—all these nasty patches of environment can play host to a misplayed golf ball. We have been there.

And others have been there before us. All but buried in the sun-dried mud of a bygone spring day, an ancient cut-up Acushnet glimmers to catch the golfer's cruising eye. Or perhaps, in a patch of low-lying, seldom-visited bog, a waffle-patterned gutta-percha antique comes to light, browned on its underside by years of exposure to the slow-acting acids of Mother Earth. For every lost ball, there was a forlorn search, perfunctory or thorough; these questing ghosts haunt the course, hovering at the juncture of their interrupted game. "Found it!" one wants to cry out in triumph, though the loser has been decades in his grave. Golf thus leaves a residue, thin but detectable, on the hundreds of acres set aside for play. Not only lost golf balls but broken tees, detached cleats, withered gloves, and the occasional broken shaft, petulantly snapped in two, mingle their mournful testimony with the silent turf.

A player interacts with the landscape at a visceral level, his natural difficulties translating into rage and even tears. At times, analyzing the niceties of a "close lie," he takes a worm's-eye view of the ball as it nestles amid pebbles and tufts; at others, his eye soars like that of a lordly hawk, seeking the telltale glint of his ball in a wide, wind-whitened world of rough. Goose feathers and dandelion polls and balled-up Kleenexes cruelly tease him with optical illusions. Nature is his companion, but, like a nagging wife, she persistently points out his inadequacies and cloaks her scenic beauties in the ongoing quarrel of the game itself. We struggle to experience the course as something other than an enemy challenging and taunting us at every swing—to experience it instead as a site of seduction, of artful landscaping, of birdsong and wild berry and pale blossom and scarlet autumnal leaf, all tamed to our use in an enchanted blend of natural creation and human recreation. But a greenside bunker pounces on a singing 9-iron and shatters our mood, narrowing our perspective to a square foot of damp sand.

The camera of Charles Lindsay knows how to see the game. It not only sees the variety of turf and the luxuriant obduracy of rough but it hears the *plip* of the sadly underclubbed approach as it sends out the ripples from its irrevocable submersion, and it smells the tonic freshness of morning dew and rising mist, and it feels the effort of a sand wedge digging deep to lift the ball over the trap's hairy, tawny lip. From Ireland to Arizona and back his camera has journeyed to record golf's sensations—the weave of interlocking incident that makes up a round. Some golf balls are lost, and with the things now retailing for twenty dollars for a sleeve of three Pro V-1s, this borders on tragedy. But some are found, right where we thought we had looked a half dozen times before. Not only is the ball ours (a theatrical examination, *sans touche,* confirms it) but it is sitting up on a bed of pine needles. There is an opening back to the fairway. There is even a shot—a long shot, with a deliberate slice, cunningly controlled—at the green. So keep your head down and swing easy. Golf may not be a lost cause after all.

WARNING SIGN, OTWAY GOLF CLUB, LETTERKENNEY, COUNTY DONEGAL, NORTHERN IRELAND

BATTERED GUTTA-PERCHA BALL, CIRCA 1890, IN THE DUNES AT ST. ANDREWS, FIFE, SCOTLAND

OLD WORLD

PLAYING YANKED DRIVES AT ST. ANDREWS, 1ST HOLE ON THE OLD COURSE, ROYAL AND ANCIENT CLUBHOUSE IN THE BACKGROUND, FIFE, SCOTLAND

The uglier a man's legs are, the better he plays golf.
It's almost a law.

—H. G. Wells

FENCED 1ST GREEN AT THE PRIMITIVE NINE-HOLE COURSE WHERE CATTLE ROAM, BARRA GOLF CLUB, ISLE OF BARRA, SCOTLAND
OPPOSITE: HIGHLAND SHEPHERD WITH CIRCA 1870 GOLF CLUB, SPOTTED NEAR DURNESS, NORTHERN SCOTLAND

Playing golf is like chasing a quinine pill around a cow pasture.

—Winston Churchill

FOX-CHEWED GOLF BALL FOUND AT CARNE GOLF LINKS, COUNTY MAYO, IRELAND

"FORESOME" ON THE PAR-THREE 15TH HOLE, ST. ENODOC GOLF CLUB, CORNWALL, ENGLAND

PETER ON HIS KNEES AFTER A TERRIBLE DRIVE, ANCIENT FAIRWAY MOWER IN FOREGROUND, 2ND HOLE ON THE NINE-HOLE COURSE AT DURNESS, SCOTLAND
OPPOSITE: EXTREME ROUGH, 2ND HOLE, NO. 1 (OLD COURSE), GULLANE GOLF CLUB, EAST LOTHIAN, SCOTLAND

It is statute and ordained that in na place
of the Realme there be used Fute-ball,
Golfe, or uther sik unproffitable sportes.

—James IV of Scotland, 1491

SIGN AT THE 18TH HOLE, ELIE GOLF HOUSE CLUB, ELIE, SCOTLAND

GOLFER AND COCKER SPANIELS, 2ND HOLE, BALLINDALLOCH CASTLE GOLF COURSE, BANFFSHIRE, SCOTLAND

In what is one of the most famous lost balls in modern sports, Tiger Woods watched as his opening drive at the 2003 British Open was swallowed in the fescue grass at Royal St. Georges. Woods went back to the first tee, took a two-stroke penalty, and hit again, finishing the tournament two off the lead to winner and then-unknown Ben Curtis. The ball was eventually found and allegedly sold for a tidy sum.

TIGER WOODS NIKE BALL, 1ST HOLE, ROYAL ST. GEORGES, KENT, ENGLAND

SEVERELY ERRANT SHOT INTO FOURTEENTH-CENTURY CASTLE RUINS, 8TH HOLE AT PENNARD GOLF CLUB, SWANSEA, WALES

"THE HIMALAYAS" AT ST. ENODOC GOLF CLUB, 8TH HOLE, CORNWALL, ENGLAND

There is no shape nor size of body, no awkwardness nor ungainliness, which puts good golf beyond reach. There are good golfers with spectacles, with one eye, with one leg, even with one arm. In golf, while there is life there is hope.

—Sir Walter Simpson, *The Art of Golf*, 1887

IN THE FAMOUS BUNKER AT NO. 4, ROYAL ST. GEORGES, KENT, ENGLAND

PREVIOUS PAGES: PONIES ON THE COURSE, 7TH HOLE AT PENNARD GOLF CLUB, SWANSEA, WALES
ABOVE: PROTECTED GREEN AT THE PAR-FOUR 11TH HOLE, CARNE GOLF LINKS, COUNTY MAYO, IRELAND

NEXT TEE, DIRECTIONS TO THE 9TH HOLE AT PENNARD GOLF CLUB, SWANSEA, WALES

SNAILS IN THE ROUGH, INSPECTING LOST *RAW DISTANCE* BALL, PAR-FIVE 6TH HOLE, OLD HEAD GOLF LINKS, COUNTY CORK, IRELAND

PAR-FOUR 14TH HOLE, BALLYBUNION GOLF CLUB, COUNTY KERRY, IRELAND

GRAVEYARD

MEMBERS/VISITORS ARE KINDLY
ASKED TO DESIST FROM
ENTERING THE GRAVEYARD TO
RETRIEVE GOLF BALLS.

YOUR CO-OPERATION IN THIS
MATTER IS GREATLY APPRECIATED.

BY ORDER COMMITTEE

GRAVEYARD, 1ST AND 14TH HOLES, BALLYBUNION GOLF CLUB, COUNTY KERRY, IRELAND

Twice in 2003 players' drives for the 3rd and 4th holes, which cross each other here, collided in midair. Never heard of that before. And a Dutchman renting a place across the street from the 4th or 5th sued for eighty thousand pounds when a golfer's shot went over the fence and took out his teeth.

—Tom Houlihan, Caddie, Ballybunion, Ireland

OPPOSITE: BALL ON THE WALL, PAR-FOUR 8TH HOLE AT CONNEMARA GOLF CLUB, COUNTY GALWAY, IRELAND
ABOVE: *INTRUDER* BALL, KENMARE GOLF CLUB, COUNTY KERRY, IRELAND

LOST BALL, PAR-FOUR 17TH HOLE, ROSAPENNA GOLF CLUB, SANDY HILL LINKS (NEW COURSE), COUNTY DONEGAL, IRELAND

REVELATION BALL, FOUND AT MURIFIELD GOLF CLUB (THE HONOURABLE COMPANY OF EDINBURGH GOLFERS), EAST LOTHIAN, SCOTLAND

FATHER KEVIN IN THE TINY BUNKER AT THE PAR-THREE 16TH, CARNE GOLF LINKS, COUNTY MAYO, IRELAND

Last year the ravens took a total of seventy-two balls out of play in a single day. They come every year and sit on a hump behind the green. If you see the ravens take your ball, you get a free drop. If the fox takes your ball, you get a free drop, and you get a free drop from rabbit scrapes or burrows.

—James O'Hara, Secretary, Carne Golf Links

RABBIT HOLE (DROP ZONE), PAR-FOUR 11TH HOLE, CARNE GOLF LINKS, COUNTY MAYO, IRELAND

WANKER BALL, FOUND IN THE ROUGH AT ST. ENODOC GOLF CLUB, CORNWALL, ENGLAND

DISCARDED GOLF SHOES IN THE CEMETERY AT ST. ENODOC GOLF CLUB, ALONG THE 11TH HOLE, CORNWALL, ENGLAND

Golf is a day spent in a round of strenuous idleness.

—William Wordsworth

Greg Norman

My favorite story involving a lost golf ball:

It was the AT&T Pebble Beach National Pro-Am, sometime in the late 1980s. I remember it as much for one extraordinary recovery shot by Jack Lemmon as I do for my own quest for the trophy.

I was paired with my good friend Clint Eastwood, and we were playing alongside the comedic duo of Jack Lemmon and Peter Jacobsen, whose missed-cut streak was already well documented. It was evident that all of Jack's time spent on the range was not paying dividends.

Not, that is, until the 16th hole at Cypress Point. This striking par-three requires a 200-yard carry across a portion of sea to a small green. There's water beyond, bunkers to surmount, and a great deal of ice plant to contend with if you are not accurate. Strong winds often prevail, making it arguably one of the toughest holes in the world. Only three golfers have had a hole-in-one here, and, ironically, Bing Crosby is a member of that famous threesome.

Well, it was the ice plant that gobbled up Jack's tee ball, and for the life of me I thought the ball was a casualty, certain never to be found, let alone played. Well, Jack wasn't about to concede. He was ready to employ a search committee and spend the allotted five minutes looking for that ball.

He stumbled upon it and, unbeknownst to the three of us, trekked down a perilously steep embankment at the water's edge and started his pre-shot routine. Clint was the first member of the rescue team to arrive on the scene, and he grabbed Jack by the back of his trousers. This was merely an effort to stabilize him, I think, or maybe to keep him from tumbling into the white caps below. I quickly assessed the situation and thought I too might be able to lend a hand, so I headed over and grabbed onto Clint.

Peter was right behind me and added one last rung to the human chain we had formed.

Jack kept going as though nothing was out of the ordinary. He took a mighty whack at the ball, which happened to be sitting up pretty well. If you haven't played out of ice plant before, one thing you have to know is that it's essential to hit the ball first. If you dig your club into the vegetation, you're done. Jack managed his best swing of the week. The ball popped right out of that thicket and came to rest just off the edge of the green.

Here's where things got messy. Jack was just far enough from the hole that he wanted to use an iron for the next shot instead of putting it, which would have been much safer. His entire upper body lifted up on that chip before he made contact, and the ball scurried off the clubface way too hard and bounded right down into the ocean! All that effort in the ice plant for nothing. He threw in the towel after the errant chip and didn't even post a score on the hole.

Moral of the story? Sometimes you're better off letting a lost ball stay lost.

NEW WORLD

BENNI THE BULL RIDER AND FRIENDS ON THE 8TH TEE, KILLDEER GOLF CLUB, NORTH DAKOTA
OPPOSITE: PULLED DRIVES, SAGUARO CACTUS, TROON GOLF CLUB, 18TH HOLE, SCOTTSDALE, ARIZONA

OPPOSITE: BALL HUNTER, PAR-THREE 17TH HOLE, OLD TABBY LINKS, SPRING ISLAND, SOUTH CAROLINA
ABOVE: YELLOW SLIDER TURTLE, 17TH GREEN, OLD TABBY LINKS, SPRING ISLAND, SOUTH CAROLINA

IN THE MARSH, PAR-FIVE 18TH HOLE, OLD TABBY LINKS, SPRING ISLAND, SOUTH CAROLINA

Got more dirt than ball. Here we go again. . . .

—Alan Shepard, *Apollo 14* Commander, preparing to take
another swing during his famous moon walk in 1971

SAND SHOT, PAR-FOUR 2ND HOLE, OCEAN COURSE, KIAWAH ISLAND, SOUTH CAROLINA

OPPOSITE: BALL HUNTER IN THE AZALEAS AT AN EXCLUSIVE GEORGIA COURSE
ABOVE: CIRCA 1905 *PLUTO* BALL IN THE WOODS, 14TH HOLE, MYOPIA HUNT CLUB, HAMILTON, MASSACHUSETTS

LEO WITH HIS BALL UP ON THE POOL SCREEN AT MY DAD'S HOUSE, 10TH HOLE, MONARCH COUNTRY CLUB, PALM CITY, FLORIDA

It's good sportsmanship not to pick up lost
golf balls while they are still rolling.

—Mark Twain

CHRIS RETRIEVING HIS BALL, GATOR APPROACHING, BETWEEN THE 17TH AND 18TH HOLES, OLD TABBY LINKS, SPRING ISLAND, SOUTH CAROLINA

LOST-BALL ZONE AND TRICERATOPS TRACK, PAR-FIVE 11TH HOLE, FOSSIL TRACE GOLF CLUB, GOLDEN, COLORADO
OPPOSITE: 11TH FAIRWAY, FOSSIL TRACE GOLF CLUB, GOLDEN, COLORADO

RATTLESNAKE ENCOUNTER, 12TH HOLE, TROON GOLF CLUB, SCOTTSDALE, ARIZONA

SANDHILL CRANE ENCOUNTER, 10TH HOLE, MONARCH COUNTRY CLUB, PALM CITY, FLORIDA
OPPOSITE: TOUGH SAND SHOT, 14TH GREEN, OCEAN COURSE, KIAWAH ISLAND, SOUTH CAROLINA

RED-TAILED HAWK'S NEST, 9TH HOLE, BETHPAGE BLACK COURSE, BETHPAGE, NEW YORK

RETRIEVING A BALL FROM THE LIVE OAK BY THE 8TH GREEN, OLD TABBY LINKS, SPRING ISLAND, SOUTH CAROLINA

MARAUDING RACCOON, 8TH HOLE, YELLOWSTONE CLUB, BIG SKY, MONTANA
OVERLEAF: BOBBY LOOKING FOR HIS SHOT ON THE PAR-FOUR 3RD HOLE, MEADOW CLUB, MARIN COUNTY, CALIFORNIA

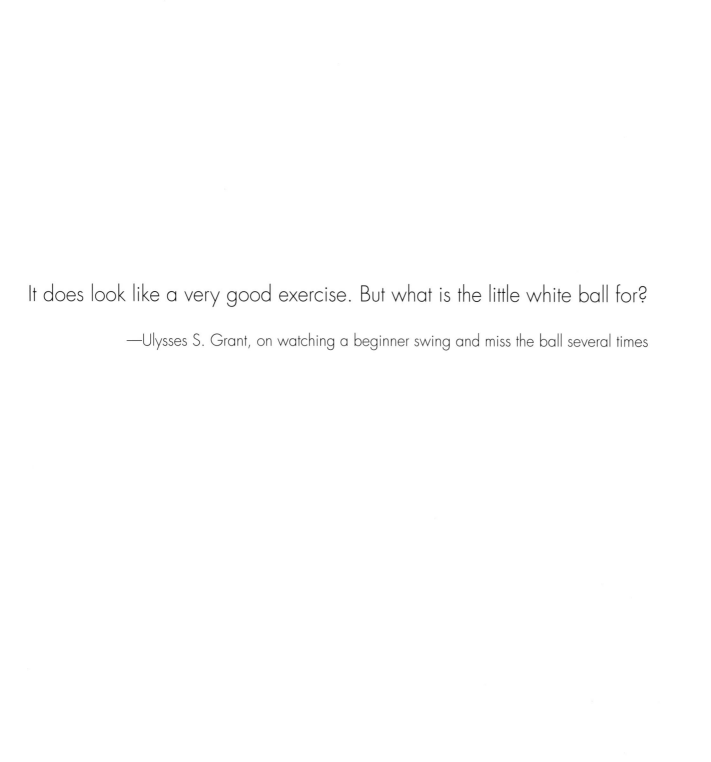

It does look like a very good exercise. But what is the little white ball for?

—Ulysses S. Grant, on watching a beginner swing and miss the ball several times

DEEP BUNKER SHOT, 11TH HOLE, PACIFIC DUNES GOLF COURSE, BANDON, OREGON

RED-TAILED HAWK BY THE PAR-THREE 15TH GREEN, CYPRESS POINT, CALIFORNIA

BLACKTAIL DEER IN RUT, PAR-THREE 3RD HOLE, SPYGLASS HILL GOLF COURSE, PEBBLE BEACH, CALIFORNIA

Golf is good for the soul. You get so mad at yourself you forget to hate your enemies.

—Will Rogers

FIRE ANTS IN THE SAND, 12TH HOLE, OLD MARSH GOLF CLUB, PALM BEACH, FLORIDA
OPPOSITE: PAR-FOUR 3RD HOLE AT BLUE LAKES COUNTRY CLUB, SNAKE RIVER CANYON, TWIN FALLS, IDAHO

WOLF SIGHTING, PAR-THREE 3RD HOLE, YELLOWSTONE CLUB, BIG SKY, MONTANA

The Montana State Department of Fish and Wildlife is advising golfers to take extra precautions and to be on the alert for bears while in the Gallatin, Helena, and Lewis and Clark National Forests area golf courses. They advise golfers to wear noise-producing devices such as little bells on their clothing to alert but not startle the bears. They also advise carrying pepper spray in case of an encounter with a bear.

It is also a good idea to watch for signs of bear activity. Golfers should be able to recognize the difference between black-bear and grizzly-bear droppings on the golf course. Black-bear droppings are smaller and contain berries and possibly squirrel fur. Grizzly bear droppings have golf balls in them and smell like pepper spray.

—Humorous advisory circulating on the Internet

GRIZZLY SCAT CONTAINING HIKER'S BELL AND GOLF BALLS, FOUND IN AN UNDISCLOSED ROCKY MOUNTAIN LOCATION

GRIZZLY ENCOUNTER ON THE 9TH GREEN, YELLOWSTONE CLUB, BIG SKY, MONTANA

Playing in the 1973 Heritage Classic in Hilton Head, South Carolina, Hale Irwin hit a wildly off-target shot that sailed into the gallery and somehow wound up in a spectator's bra. Golf rules stipulate that a player should personally remove the ball from any such obstruction and drop it without penalty. In this case an exception was made: the woman chose to remove the ball herself. Irwin took the free drop and played on.

ALOHA, MAUI BALL, FOUND ON THE 18TH HOLE, PLANTATION COURSE, KAPALUA GOLF CLUB, LAHAINA, HAWAII
OPPOSITE: BRAZILIAN RED-CAP CARDINALS ON THE 9TH GREEN, KO'OLAU GOLF CLUB, OAHU, HAWAII

Ko'olau Golf Course in Hawaii is considered the toughest course in the nation. The back tees have a slope rating of 162. The course encompasses three distinct climate zones with extreme elevation changes. The lowest score recorded there is 68. The most lost balls by one individual in one round, 63.

ABANDONED SHOT, 12TH HOLE, KO'OLAU GOLF CLUB, OAHU, HAWAII

DIVOTS ON THE TEE BOX AT THE PAR-THREE 11TH HOLE, PLANTATION COURSE, KAPALUA, HAWAII
OPPOSITE: PEDE IN HIS GREEK MILITARY UNIFORM AND SON BILL, 17TH HOLE, EL BORRACHO TOURNAMENT, THE SANCTUARY, SEDALIA, COLORADO

Golf is, in part, a game; but only in part. It is also in part a religion, a fever, a vice, a mirage, a frenzy, a fear, an abscess, a joy, a thrill, a pest, a disease, an uplift, a brooding, a melancholy, a dream of yesterday, and a hope for tomorrow.

—*New York Tribune*, 1916

19TH-HOLE ANTICS AT THE EL BORRACHO TOURNAMENT, 1ST TEE, THE SANCTUARY, SEDALIA, COLORADO

Charles Lindsay

Golf is a curious vice. Satisfaction isn't guaranteed—it's fleeting at best—but the addiction is insidious and sure. What can we expect from a sport where the absolute best in the world regularly screw up?

My perspective on the game is not the one seen in books and calendars of players with perfect swings on impossibly great courses in exotic locales. Not the straight-down-the-middle approach. Gigantic hooks and pushes take me into ankle-deep muck, far from the fairway, fighting the sagebrush, dodging the poison ivy, and looking for a white orb as round as the moon and equally uninterested in my predicament. The six handicap of my youth has grown huge through decades of neglect. The concept for *Lost Balls* evolved from the depths of this realization, not so much a sharing of misery as a celebration of it.

The golf shot, with its aspiration, trajectory, and distance, seems to mirror human ambition, to take measure of our successes and failures. Of course those who don't play see only the surface details: ricocheting balls, mammoth mowers, cowering onlookers, and loud, angry men wearing funny clothes, their clubs flailing, speaking a language all their own. But there is so much more to the game, its history, culture, and interaction with nature. I decided that a different story could be told.

Obviously I'm not the only hacker around. So I started looking out-of-bounds, outside the box, for what certain pleasure must be there. In swamps, dunes, deserts, and woods across America, I found hundreds of golf balls, a full century of future stratigraphy, the detritus of wishful players' misplaced hopes and of an enormously fertile industry. I smiled as the wildlife cautiously observed me as I photographed, an ambassador from the upright species that pelts their territory. And as I looked over my shoulder on the way back to the green, I often wondered if Mother Nature was in fact mocking me.

POSSIBLY THE WORLD'S OLDEST GOLF BALL, MADE OF BOXWOOD WITH A LEAD CENTER, EXCAVATED IN 2003 FROM AN EARLY SIXTEENTH-CENTURY TRASH HEAP. THE CLUB HEAD FOUND NEARBY WAS CARBON-DATED TO 1432. COLLECTION OF JOSEPH R. TISCORNIA

Everywhere there are lost golf balls—stuck up in trees, lodged in birds' nests, embedded in cacti, gathering on coral reefs, and layering the wetlands like *Hansel and Gretel* cookie-crumb messages left to be deciphered. In the course of my hunting, I discovered a curious language on the balls themselves, a veritable Rosetta Stone of knowledge: *Pluto, Bambi, Long and Straight, Wanker,* and *Revelation.* I met collectors of rare and antique golf balls—who knew they existed?—and even had a chance to photograph what may be the oldest golf ball in the world.

I traveled to Ireland and then on to Scotland, where pagan shepherds once whacked rocks into rabbit holes and where my forebears came from. There the game is played quickly, in wind and weather, closer to nature, closer to sheep. But even if golf's roots are in the heather and earth, hazards with names such as Hell's Half Acre, the Devil's Asshole, and the Church Pews often make it seem more like navigating a Protestant-inspired minefield laced with opportunities for sin and redemption in the Garden of Eden.

I dutifully read a stack of books with titles such as *Zen Golf This* and *Tiger Says That,* searching for knowledge and a cure for my ailing game. My wife smirked as the pile of books grew. But there were no miracles—rather an ongoing tug-of-war between strokes of genius and far more frequent disappoint-ments. The game of golf challenged my healthy sense of self-esteem. In photography you edit out the bad shots; in golf you're condemned to live with them. Still, I wondered, how difficult can it possibly be?

Murphy's Law and quantum physics agree that almost nothing in life behaves as you'd like it to—not children, politicians, or pets, and least of all a small white ball destined for a distant hole in the ground. So perhaps the true gift that golf offers us is the time spent with friends and in nature—the more nature the better—in a state of perpetual folly, witnessing one another's strengths and shortcomings and humans' tendency to behave like beasts.

It seems likely that leisure sports evolved from Neanderthal combat and hunting. In golf there is no life or death; the dangers are mainly errant balls and battered egos. Yet, like a spear placed perfectly behind a mammoth's shoulder blade, a great golf shot is something to behold, something to seek, seemingly at any cost. Which is why we keep swinging, groaning, practicing, and shaking our fists at the all-too-rare miracle of the perfect shot.

There is a golf ball on the moon, left behind by Alan Shepard, but I hear the course isn't very well maintained.

Concentrate, align, exhale, focus, slowly now, *whoosh* . . . fore!

DRIVING RANGE, SPYGLASS HILL GOLF COURSE, PEBBLE BEACH, CALIFORNIA

ACKNOWLEDGMENTS

Many people helped and encouraged me during the making of this book. My heartfelt thanks go out to each of them. From the beginning, my wife, Catherine Chalmers, and my editor, Michael Sand, offered enthusiastic support and invaluable advice. Thanks to Miko McGinty for designing the book. At Bulfinch, thanks to Karen Murgolo, Matthew Ballast, Jason Bartholomew, Claire Greenspan, Eveline Chao, and Alyn Evans for their contributions. Thanks to Bulfinch publisher Jill Cohen for her confidence in the idea.

Joellen Zeh at Audubon International was very helpful with introductions to courses involved in their Signature and Sanctuary programs, which promote environmental stewardship for golf courses—a great cause. Thanks also to Kevin Fletcher. For more information, please visit www.audubonintl.org.

John Updike was onboard early in the project, and that meant a great deal to me. Thanks to Jamie and Dick Purinton, who arranged the introduction. John said the kindest things when I repeatedly hooked into the woods! Thanks to Greg Norman and his manager, Brian Stevens, for providing lively text.

A series of introductions and subsequent meetings arose from a complete stranger, now a friend, who glimpsed several old golf balls in my camera bag while I was clearing security at West Palm Beach airport. Jeff Jung spoke up, we flew together to New York, and soon I was in touch with collectors, historians, and certifiable characters: Rick Hartbrought, Joseph Tiscornia, Dick Estey, and Dr. David Malcolm. Enormous thanks to all of you. What a pleasure.

Josephine and Jerry Quinlan at Celtic Golf helped arrange my cars in Ireland and Scotland. My father was one of their first clients, and his trips with Celtic Golf were among his most memorable times. For more on them, visit www.celticgolf.com.

In Scotland, thanks to Lord and Lady Marnoch for the morning spent salmon fishing on the Deveron and the golf at Nairn and Murifield. Thanks to Gavin Hepburn for advice that led to the wonderful meeting in high winds at Durness with the Allinghams, David,

Annie, Peter, and their golf comrade Jude De Souza. That encounter led to many laughs and fine photos. Thanks to Sandy Rhigolter, who ran his sheep on Sunday morning! Thanks to Oliver Russell and Maurice Gibson at Ballindalloch Castle. Thanks to Kate Dolan, Violet Haig, Maureen Parry, Maris Maccrossan, and Bob MacAlindin at Lundin Ladies Golf Club. Thanks to Patricia Savin at North Berwick and to Alasdair Good—Head PGA Pro at Gullane Golf Club.

Further south, thanks to David Lane, Doug Smallman, Christopher Gabbey, Matthew Arnold, and Andrew Carney at Royal St. Georges. Thanks to Dewi and Hazel Lloyd and Mike Bennett at Pennard, and to Nick Williams and Chris Worlidge, whom I met at St. Enodoc.

In Ireland, thanks to John McLaughlin at North and West Coast Links, to Fiona McDonald and Michael Kellehe at Old Head, Brian Shaw at Doonbeg Golf Club, Frank Casey at Rossepenna Hotel & Golf Links, Eoin Behan at Connemara Links, Shauna McVeigh at Royal County Down. I had the most amazing time at Carne Golf Links. Thanks to James O'Hara, Eamon Mangan, Edmund McAndrew, Gary Stanley, Father Kevin Hegarty, P. J. Carey, and Peter Mulry. Thanks to Larry Schnell for the fox-chewed ball! While there I met Jim Engh, golf-course architect extraordinaire. That meeting led to shoots in the U.S. at Fossil Trace, The Sanctuary, Hawk Tree, Killdeer, and Black Rock. Jim, thanks for sharing your vision.

In the United States, special thanks to Spring Island, The Sanctuary, and The Yellowstone Club for exceptional hospitality. At Spring Island, thanks to Glenys Ryan, Jim and Betsy Chaffin, Bill Sampson, and Seth Zeigler. Thanks also to photographer Chris Lane for help with the turtles and gators, and to Rob Brown for letting me catch a lift on the cherry picker. At The Sanctuary, thanks to Dave Liniger, Rudy Zupetz, Pete and Bill Maniatis, John Cullen, Peaches, and the entire El Borracho Tournament gang. At The Yellowstone Club, thanks to Tim, Edra, and Beau Blixseth, Steve Satterstrom, Hank Kashiwa, Tim Foote, and Rich Jorgenson. Bear hugs and BIG thanks to Ed George, Tracy Krueger, and Troy Hyde at Animals of Montana.

My father-in-law and dear friend Jim Chalmers got himself into the mysterious azaleas while in Georgia, where we were in training at Road Atlanta for this year's mandatory high-speed auto travel. Thanks, Jim!

Thanks to Dr. Hank Ramini for the day at Salem Country Club. Thanks to James Brown at Bandon and Pacific Dunes (on the jacket). Thanks to Al King for the introduction to North Dakota, also Benni Paulson, Dennis Hartman, and Greg Andersen at Killdeer. Thanks to David Heroian at the Myopia Hunt Club,

Drew Annan and Tony Shuster at Forest Highlands, Mark Clark at Troon Golf Club, Jim Colo at Old Marsh, Connie Norwood at the PGA Learning Center, Jim Hajek and Jimmy Mul at Fossil Trace, Terry Cook at Spyglass, Ken Nice at Bandon Dunes, raptor biologist Jim Jones and Long Island Power Authority bucket-truck operator Gary Steedman for help up in the oaks at Bethpage, Joel Waller and Tim Obenchain at Blue Lakes Country Club, Frank Contey at The Tuxedo Club, Art Kerrick and Doyle Corbett at Sun Valley, Rob Nelson at Ko'olau Golf Club, Craig Trenholm, Marty Keiter, and Liz Marquez at Kapalua (Plantation Course), Victoria Cabiles at Manele Bay, Island of Lana'i, Jim O'Neal at Meadow Club, Mike Vegas at Kiawah Island, Ocean Course. Thanks to Bob Ford at Seminole Golf Club and Oakmont Country Club, and Adam Brigham at Oakmont Country Club. Thanks to Emily Taylor for help with the rattlesnake.

Thanks to my golf pals, who have endured my erratic game: Red Mathews, Leo Nentwig, Rich Miller, Hal Greene, Jeff Brotman, Bobby Locke, Geoff Isles, Richard Prince, John and Randy Ashton, Mindy Mays, Lincoln Potter, Sharon, Zoe, and Terry Reid, Mike McCollum, and to PGA Golf Professional Rick Martino for his heroic attempts to help me! Thanks to Dave Faltings and Terry Ring at Silver Creek Outfitters in Ketchum, Idaho, for getting me out fishing—a temporary but necessary break from golf. Thanks to Ray Merritt for legal advice and to Joan Beck, my perfect travel agent. In Rensselaerville, thanks to my great friend Alberto Caputo for immoral support, to Victor Schrager for helpful advice, and to Dudley Reed for my author photo and other comedies.

Ken Horowitz, Juan Cisneros, and Bob Cattan at Ken Horowitz Photographic Services in New York are a pleasure to work with. Thanks, guys.

Thanks to Jeff Karp at Rolleiflex USA for the assistance with all my camera equipment.

For information concerning my limited-edition photographs, commissions, and exhibitions, please visit www.lostballs.net or e-mail info@lostballs.net. For more information about my previous books and works in progress, please visit www.charleslindsay.com.